The Jezebel Spirit
(Pocket Size)

The Jezebel Spirit (Pocket Size)

TACTICS OF JEZEBEL'S CONTROL

Bill Vincent

RWG Publishing

CONTENTS

RWG Publishing

PO Box 596

Litchfield, IL 62056

https://rwgpublishing.com/

Published in the United States of America

1

Introduction

Revelations chapter 2:20, nevertheless, I have this against you. You have tolerated the woman Jezebel, who calls herself a prophetess, by her teaching, she misleads my servants into sexual immorality, in eating food sacrificed to idols. I have given her time to repent for her immorality, but she is unwilling. So, I will cast her on the bed of suffering, and I will make those that commit adultery with her suffer intensely unless they repent of her ways.

We never talk about witchcraft, but we experience it daily, but the church is just so spiritually numb. The church is so spiritually immature that you don't realize that you are experiencing witch-craft daily because you've just diagnosed it as anxiety. You've just called it fear, and you call it depression, and so then what we end up doing is that we begin to look to other sources to help us fight spiritual warfare instead of the word of God.

Witchcraft is real. Do you know that? Check in your spirit that little discernment that you've got a funny feeling, and you don't understand why you have a funny feeling, and it doesn't make sense. That's the caution of the Holy Spirit. It's like when they ask you, hey, do you want to come in? And you're on that third day, and you know you shouldn't go in there, that little check in your spirit.

That is a discernment check.

When you begin to expose the Jezebel spirit, it's like flipping on a light. It's like just complete understanding, a realization of what you're facing.

First things first, when we're dealing with the Jezebel spirit. Historically, unfortunately, the Jezebel Spirit's been used to control women in the church, and it's interesting because, as we've seen, these women marches that have been going on in the country, in the nation, watching this evil act on

TV. I saw women dressing up like anatomy parts and cursing, dressing up as warriors and cursing, and swearing and chanting.

I'm looking at this, and up in my spirit said, this is 'Jezebelic.' You got to be able to discern the spirits. People shouldn't march for some things and don't align yourself with a foul spirit because you just ruined your cause by uniting with Jezebel, and Jezebel is using you. So, hear me clearly, but I'm exposing what's been going on.

Listen, the Jezebel spirit is not to control you. It's not to silence you. It's not to control people. So, when I'm talking about the Jezebel spirit, I'm not talking about the eccentric lady that's in the church. No, that's not what I'm talking about. The next thing is, just because you have a characteristic. The Jezebel spirit operates in both men and women. It's not only specific to females. One thing that I found is how many more men operated in the spirit due to the demasculinization of men in society. So, it's not gender-specific.

Just because you have a characteristic of Jezebel doesn't mean that you have given over to it. I'm going to go over many of these characteristics in this book, but just because you identify with the characteristic of Jezebel does not mean that Jezebel spirit has fully possessed you, or just because you have one characteristic or more. But if you have multiple of Jezebel's attributes in operation in your life, you need to do a great self-evaluation on who you're truly submitted to. This will tell if you are a true disciple and a good follower of Jesus Lord.

So, if you're afraid that you have characteristics and that's a good thing, this is because your heart isn't given over to this foul spirit.

It's not gender-specific. Number two, Jezebel doesn't like to be talked about. And I got a lot of people that will play this down. Oh, look at those charismatic Pentecostals and their Jezebel spirit, as they're living in complete bondage.

Number three. This is very important. We're not on a witch hunt. Put your sword away. You don't have to find it, your Jezebel will find you. You don't have to look across the room at church and wonder, these kids, I wonder if the guy with ripped jeans, I wonder if he has...No, you don't have to do that. You don't have to find it. It's going to find you.

Now, what is that Jezebel Spirit? Jezebel Spirit is modern-day witchcraft. The spirit of Jezebel is a demonic power-hungry spirit that uses witchcraft to control God's people and God's church. This is a seductive political and religious spirit that targets prophetic spirit-led soul-winning people in ministries. The divisive spirit attempts to destroy lives, families, ministries, and close friends.

Above all, the spirit of Jezebel will stop at nothing until you abandon the call of God on your life. The people of God are tolerant of it because we are ignorant. The spirit of Jezebel sounds like this. If you want to summarize it in a word, to give up, quit, or abandon the call of God on your life. The purpose of the Jezebel spirit is that you will give up on the call of God on your life. You will give up on ministry. You will give up on your church. You will give up on your marriage. You'll give up on your family. That's what this is to kill the future and the destiny that you're called to live out.

Who was Jezebel? We find the woman Jezebel in 1st Kings. She was the seductive prophetess of the false God, Baal. Baal was the arch-enemy of Yahweh, or the God of Israel, our God, Jehovah. Baal was in direct opposition to God. Jezebel was the daughter of the King priest Sidon named Ethbaal. We find that in 1st Kings Chapter 16. Jezebel means, without dwelling or cohabitation, unmarried, uncommitted, or unhusbanded. Jezebel will not submit. Let me say that again. Jezebel will not submit.

The spirit that's in America right now that will not submit, it's Jezebel in operation. There's a new thing I've seen all over social media called the resistance that whatever the government does, they're going to resist it. This is a spirit that's in operation. As Christians, we're supposed to pray for our leaders. Now, if there's absolute demonic, evil going on, we need to address it. But, interestingly, we're not addressing the genocide of abortion. I no longer see Christians all up in arms, marching, and protesting for gay marriage. Christians have been quiet.

I'm telling you, it is a spirit in operation that is going on in America right now, this spirit will not submit. It refuses to live in peaceful cohabitation. When Ahab, the reigning King of Israel, married Jezebel, he directly aligned God's people with God's enemy. So, if you know your Bible, Ahab was the King of Israel. Jezebel was the daughter of the high priest of Baal. Jezebel's father mentored her, and Ahab married this heathen goddess of Baal. So, he directly aligns God's people who are called to serve Yahweh. And now, he married her, and he's in Alliance with evil. Are you here? So, Jezebel is now at the helm, influencing the King of God's people.

Let's keep going. So, the high priest personally mentored his daughter in the worship of the pagan God of sexuality and spiritual war. Ethbaal means man of Baal or Baal is with him. So, the King devoted his entire life to the worship of Baal, teaching his daughter how to do it. Her goddess of fertility is not only the giver of life, but also the giver of death. He gave her the assignment to bring death and destruction to all those who oppose Baal, thus, naming her Jezebel. Jezebel also worshipped Astarte or Ashtaroth, the Canaanite goddess of fertility called Ishtar. She was regarded as the goddess of love and sensual pleasure. Listen, when the world is saying that we need love, they're not talking about the God of love.

God's definition of love isn't to have sex with whoever you want. God's definition of love is obedience. I am so glad that Jesus loved us so much. He was obedient to the Father when he said, is there any other way? But he obeyed. Jesus said, if you love me, you obey me. So, when we're talking about this general word love in the world today, it's not Jesus' love.

Their gods Dagon, Baal, Ashtaroth, and Molec, combined for the erotic acts of perverted, heterosexual relationships, homosexual activity, violent sexual acts, body piercing, including genitals, body cutting, and violent sexual acts and also they had an infatuation with blood, drinking and draining and also prostitution and ceremonial orgies. Jezebel was one of the originators of child sacrifice or abortion. They're marching across America for a woman's right to murder, as the church is scared-speechless. This is a spirit that's in operation. Jezebel, who had ceremony orgies, just imagine, across the street, okay. And I know this is graphic.

Okay, so, imagine if we had church and then across the street, we had Baal's sex temple. And across the street, as we're worshiping and singing to the King of Kings and Lord of Lords. Imagine they're having sex orgies across the street, and the women of the church are prostitutes and getting pregnant with babies as we're worshiping God.

Then they take the babies that they just got impregnated with, with their orgies, and then they sacrifice them in an offering of sacrifices to Baal. This is evil? This is the spirit that's in operation in America as we've murdered over 60 million babies. Where are the marches on that? Where are the protests on that? We need more voices to stand and preach righteousness and true justice.

You study Planned Parenthood, and you study what she tried to do, strategically placing abortion clinics and tried to sterilize African American communities because they said they're cockroaches to humanity. Where's your righteous indignation there? I'm telling you, this is foul. This is a foul spirit in operation. And then, you've got Christians on the other end that wants to say that women need health. Yes, you do need health, and there are healthy options that aren't murdering innocent children.

I'm not trying to be political here. But I'm being spiritual. This is a spirit that's in operation. This is a spirit of death. It's an antichrist spirit that's come to kill, steal, and destroy. Look at the society and look at Jezebel's religion, sets up a sexual life how you want, do what you want – no boundaries. The god of love, the god of fertility, and the god of the giver of life and the taker of life. This is a foul spirit that's in operation, okay. There's so much more to this, and I've got to keep going. So, Ahab is what we're protesting. It's insane.

The leader of God's people now aligns God's people with God's enemy, and her name was Jezebel. This is what she began to do. She began to round up every true prophet, every man of God, and begin to kill them one by one. Everyone that would speak out and say this is a sin. Everyone that would stand up and say this is wrong. Everyone that would speak the truth, speak true righteousness, speak true justice was murdered. She had assassins go out and put them to the sword. So then, they had men of God hiding in caves, afraid of their life or a modern-day version of afraid of losing their 501C3.

This is what was going on. So, watch, she's getting God's people to worship Baal. Baal means master or possessor through disunity. In Ephesians chapter 5, we're described as the bride of Christ. The bride of Christ is now divorcing Yahweh to unite with Baal and this evil. It's evil. The last thing she did, guys, this is so crazy. This is insane how this applies to today. The next thing she did was that she got all of Israel to begin to worship Baal, but not just to worship Baal, but to embrace it as normal.

Listen, two-thirds of Israel was now practicing Baal worship as their practice. It became the norm. Sexual perversion became the norm. Gender identity became the norm. I'm telling you, we are living in a Romans chapter 1 era of a debased mind. Isaiah said it perfectly, in Isaiah chapter 5, he said a day would come where men will call evil good and good evil. That is the day we're living in. And if you say anything that is biblically supportive and biblically accurate, you're called hateful. This is insanity. Or, I say it this way. This is confusion.

Revelation chapter 2, We got to remember this is John, who is shipwrecked on the Island of Patmos. This is where he's given the vision of Revelation. So, this is Jesus speaking in your Bible. I know it's pink and white up there, but in your Bible, it should be red. So, Jesus is speaking in the book of Revelation, and he says this.

Nevertheless, I have this against you. You have tolerated the woman, Jezebel. I believe that marching with is toleration, it's incredible how we're told to tolerate in today's society. But God's word says, don't tolerate.

Interestingly, we are more secular than we are Christian. We are more American than we are a citizen of heaven. So, He says, don't tolerate the woman, Jezebel. So, how is Jesus talking about the woman Jezebel and when Revelations chapter 2:20 was written between 67 and 97 A.D. after Jesus' death. And in 1st Kings Chapter 18, it's approximately between 800 and 900 BC. So roughly a thousand years from the woman, Jezebel to Jesus talking about Jezebel.

Now, if you believe Genesis chapter 6, where God said, men won't live past one hundred and twenty days anymore, you know that she didn't live past one hundred and twenty days. We know that she fell out of the window when Jehu called her down, so she's not alive anymore. She fell out of the window. Dogs trample on her steps. I'm ruining the movie. Spoiler alert. So, she's dead. How can Jesus be talking about her? Because he's talking about a spirit that's in operation that we use the phrase 'Jezebel spirit' to expose the spirit and operation.

Ephesians Chapter 6:12, It says this, the struggle is not against flesh and blood, but it's against the rulers, the authorities against powers of this dark world, the spiritual forces of the heavenly realms. Some spirits are in operation to try to destroy this house. Your lives, your ministry, your marriage, and the church has to be discerning.

I'm going to list some of the characteristics of behaviors of Jezebel. Now, it's very important; the best way to do this is that you examine yourself before you try to write down the names of the people that this identifies with. That's called being healthy. So, you always apply it to you first.

Now again, I said this at the beginning, just because you exhibit a few characteristics does not mean that you are fully possessed with the Jezebel spirit. But if three or four of these hit you spot on, then you need to start being aware of what's going on in your life. Now, here's what's crazy. I'm not describing your mother-in-law, your ex-pastor, a church member, or your friend, or your boss. I'm going to describe characteristics of a spirit, but, amazingly, it will relate to different people around the world that I have never met, they're not related by blood because it's a spirit.

2

∽

Characteristics of the Jezebel Spirit

1. **Jezebel is Jealous of Everything**
   Number one, she's jealous of everything. She's extremely jealous. What is she jealous of? Anything there is to be jealous of. She'll be jealous of your marriage. I'm going to use the word 'she' to describe the spirit, but remember it's boys and girls, okay? So, she'll be jealous of your car; she'd be jealous of your house, she'd be jealous if the pastor said hi to you and not her when he didn't see the next per-

son. Be jealous. I've been serving longer than this person. How did that person get faster? How come that person's sitting in my spot? How come they're standing in my place? How come this person, it gets more likes. That person has more followers. This person has more interest. This person has better children. I'm telling you that they will be jealous of anything and everything. She's driven by this jealous nature to be better, wants what other people have.

2. **Jezebel Will not Submit**

Will not submit; her name means "won't submit." Will not submit. So many people think they're submitted because they say it, and you are saying that your life has nothing to do with submission.

We don't even know you're submitted until your will is tested. It's funny you've got social media. Social media is everybody's highlight reel. Some have a Facebook ministry. This is just posting and pushing your beliefs on others. Arguing is not a ministry. Like who except for like really weird pastors that don't understand Instagram. But nobody posts ugly pictures of themselves. You're like, Oh, my eyes are closed. I look like I am walking dead. Like, get a new one. No one posts bad pictures.

It's not what you profess with your mouth. It's the process of walking out true loyalty. Submission isn't controlled. Jezebel tries to use control. That's because she's not submitted.

Submission is a dirty word in the church – meaning don't control me. No, no submission means trust, so they don't trust you, so they don't submit to you. They do what they want. They refuse to submit. Let me repeat it, we don't know if you're submitted until your will is tested.

3. Jezebel is Very Seductive

Very seductive. This one tends to be a female trait more than a man's trait. Listen, we are living in a seductive world that sex sells everything, and the church is buying. Modesty has left the church with this day and age on the internet. It's so easy to find perversion. This is a seductive spirit. What do seductive spirits do? You need what I have. Read Proverbs chapter 7, and it describes the seductive spirit. It brings you, draws you in, and entices you.

It uses words of flattery. Man, you're way more than a man than my husband. Man, I wish I had a man like you.

I've had women email and message me on social media. They say things like, and I love the way you preach and would love to talk with you. I just block them. Why would you block her over stuff like that? Because I felt the spirit behind it. Come on, hear this. There have been so many marriages that have been destroyed by Facebook, and past friends come on somebody. It was a good thing that you lost track of them. Hear it. It's seductive, trying to seduce, trying to flirt. Listen, gentlemen, let me help you, don't flirt.

4. Jezebel Stirs up Strife

The fourth characteristic of Jezebel is that she stirs up strife. Stirs up, it's a stir. What is strife? Strife is creating discord. I'll put it like this. The Bible says that one puts a thousand a flight. Two puts 10,000, and a three-cord strand is not broken easily. So, strife is discord that breaks the chords of unity. So, strife, watch this, if you have a three cord strand, strife breaks one cord. So now, it's only two chords, so a two-chord strand cannot hold three cord strand weight. So, strife keeps a team from holding what they need to hold together, together.

Strife is like this. Strife is someone saying, man, there's something about that person that I discern. I don't know what it is. I discern it. Now, if you're discerning something, keep that to yourself until the Lord gives you the revelation of what you're discerning. Then, take it to the proper place. But if you tell someone, hey, I am discerning something about this person over here. Now, the person that you said they're going to be trying to be spiritual too, they're going to look at that person and try to discern for themselves what you're discerning. So now, they're going to be trying to find things that aren't there. You know what, that's called strife.

Now, suddenly, you'd be trying to find devils. You are trying to find instances. This spirit operates in strife, she maneuvers in strife. This is what she does. She sows seeds of discord. If you read in the New Testament, this is what the Pharisees did when they had a problem with the disciples. They went to Jesus, and when they had a problem with Jesus, they went to the disciples. That's discord. If you have a problem with someone and you're going to other people and complaining about them, that's sin, and that's discord.

5. Jezebel Starts Unsanctioned Ministries Without Permission

Number five, this one's always popular. Jezebel starts unsanctioned ministries without permission. Now, remember, she's unsubmitted, so she does what she wants. Remember, it's a he or she, but this person does what they want. And then, when they're challenged on starting their ministry without bringing it under the proper covering of the church, it's what? No, you mean the church doesn't want us to have Bible studies. How can the church not want us to read our Bible? No, the church has Bible studies, and the leaders go through proper training so that we're all in unity with the same heart and the same vision and the same voice.

So, we don't let deception come in the ranks. But then, they go around telling people; I can't believe they didn't want me to do it. And what kind of church doesn't want us to read a Bible? But the truth is you didn't take it to the proper chains because your DNA is unsubmitted. Here's the program to go through to start the Bible study. Go through it because we'll help get Jezebel out before you go, and put Jezebel in everyone in your Bible study. I can't believe they wouldn't want you, and what church would want to do that? Suddenly, I'm in the web of Jezebel.

6. Jezebel Operates in Confusion

The number six characteristic is that Jezebel operates in confusion. Isn't it fantastic how one day a person's life has never been better? God's moving their marriage is the strongest. Their kids are the best, and their kids serve God, their finances have never been better. The pastor has ministered to them so much – in worship, programs, meeting people. They're here for life. This church has saved their lives. Their marriage was on the rocks. They came to this house. God ministered and set them free. God did so much, and then have one conversation with one Jezebel. Suddenly, they want to leave the church. They want to abandon ministry. They don't know if they should be here and they're completely confused. That's a spirit.

That's how this foul spirit works and operates to bring confusion. See, when you start letting your guard down, and you let it in, then it begins to work on you. Isn't it interesting when people are struggling with their sexuality and use the word confused to describe it? The enemy operates in confusion. God is not the author of confusion. He's the author of a sound mind.

Listen, if you feel like you're in a season of being confused, you know what you need to do? Nothing. If you're lost, you don't keep driving in a random direction because why would you want to drive five minutes in the wrong direction? You hear me, and when you are confused, you know what you do? You stop, you shut up, and you pray. You worship, and you wait for the peace of God to come back and lead you. She operates in confusion.

7. Jezebel Won't Accept Apologies

Number seven. She won't accept apologies. This one got me confused for years. I remember looking back years later, and I was like, Lord, I've repented to that person a hundred times, and they keep bringing up the same thing I repented of. Why won't they forgive? I was praying. I said, Lord, explain it to me. Why won't Jezebels forgive? And the Holy Spirit said, what is forgiveness? And I said, well it's letting go. And he said of control. See, the moment they forgive you, they got to be Godly.

They have to be Christians. They have to operate in the Holy Spirit, and in the fruit of the spirit, but they don't do that. And so, they will use that against you, and they will hold on and not forgive you to control you because you feel bad that they're mad at you, and they use that to control you. They won't accept apologies.

8. Jezebel's Information is Ammunition

Number eight, information is ammunition. This one's dirty, Jezebel will ask you questions always to get you to talk, to get you to tell things, to give up information, to get you to give up secrets, to get you to give past and give up history. And she will use it and hold it and use it to shoot it back at you. So, watch, your past is your testimony until you cross her, and then she uses your past against you. This is evil. This is the accuser of the brethren stuff. This is an antichrist demonic spirit at work. The worst Jezebel that I ever dealt with was good at using things against me. Once she learned that about all the things that I had been delivered, she used them against me later.

Information is ammunition, and I can't describe it, guys. It's only demons and demonic at work. Somehow, Jezebel gets you to talk, and you talk and talk and talk and talk and talk. What do you feel about that? How do you feel about them? What did you think when the pastor said this? Then you feel like you've got the microphone and you're on the stage, and it's your time to talk, and then she gets you with it. I'm telling you, Proverbs warns about the wisdom of talking little. There's wisdom in not posting all of your feelings on social media.

There's wisdom in being prayerful in what you say. Information is ammunition.

9. Jezebel Has No Fruit

Number nine, she has no fruit. We have to break something in the church world where we call everything fruit that's not fruit, let me help you. Your car is not fruit. It's a car. Your house isn't fruit. It's a house. Those might be evidence of good investments, but it's not fruit. The only fruit is found in Galatians Chapter 5, love, joy, peace, patience, goodness, kindness, gentleness, faithfulness, and self-control. That's the only thing that's fruit. But because we don't bear fruit in the church today, we have to call things that are not fruit, fruit to make it look spiritual.

One thing about fruit is that your pastor can't

produce it for you. Your life group leader can't provide it for you. Only you can produce fruit in your life from the seeds you plant, to the watering you do through the prayer, reading, worship, and discipleship that produces God's kingdom in your life. Love, joy, peace, patience, goodness, kindness, gentleness, faithfulness, and self-control are not a part of Jezebel's lifestyle. If you do not see fruit, it should be a tall tale sign.

10. Jezebel is Never Wrong

And number 10. She is never, ever, wrong. Why? Because she's so proud because she doesn't operate in humility. So, she's never wrong. How can we be right every time? And you can't be. No one is, and if you're always right or you have to be right, then there's a deceptive spirit that's at work in your life. It's never wrong.

11. Jezebel Operates in a Fault-Finding Spirit

She operates in a fault-finding spirit. She tries to find faults that are not there. She gets you chasing fake reports and fake allegations to distract you with what she's doing. She's a fault finder. Well, you're just hardhearted. You're just not generous. You are just mean to people. No, those are all the things that she does, but she's trying to find the faults in you. That's how she uses information and ammunition against you.

These are just some of the characteristics. I gave you 11 of dozens of Jezebel's characteristics. Again, just because you have one doesn't mean that you're operating in the spirit, these are some of my high-lighted ones. If multiple of these line up with an individual, you've got to be aware that a spirit is at work. Jezebel uses witchcraft as a control. Control is witchcraft. To control people is witchcraft. Jesus didn't control anyone. He said to his disciples, hey, follow me. He said to a rich man, sell everything you had, and he let them walk away.

Do you know what pastors would do today? The Bible says in the book of Mark, it's one of those that many disciples fell away when he was talking about eating my flesh and drinking my blood. And guess what? He let them, and he turned to his disciples, says, you all are going to leave too? Listen, if people are going to leave be-cause of things, let them leave for whatever.

One excuse is as good as another. If it's not one thing, it'll be this relationship. It'd be that relation-ship. I want a church that really gives us the meat. This church has not given us the meat. Silly, rebellious people, grownups feed themselves, but if it's not this excuse, it's that excuse. It's another excuse.

3

∽

Tactics of Jezebel's Control

Jezebel works through tactics of control. Four tactics of Jezebel's control is fear, manipulation, intimidation, and domination.

1. **Fear**

   Number one, fear. Fear of threats threatens you, so you can respond to a threat rather than dealing with her. You respond to Jezebel rather than dealing with God and honoring God. Threat sounds like this. I've heard this personally. If you leave our church, you're cursed. Really? So, no matter how messed up people are, there is always one true thing. Jesus will come to heal you, set you free, and make you the righteousness of Christ. But if you leave this church, you're cursed. That is a threat.

If you leave my ministry, you're cursed. Now, don't get me wrong, a lot of people can leave long ways, and there can be great consequences for their evil behavior, but I'm talking about that fear. You're going to be destroyed. I had people that served a Jezebel that told me that if I leave that church, I'll dry up and lose all my gifts from God. It has been 9 years now, and God is still faithful. Jezebel is all about. It's everything through fear. I'm afraid of making them mad, and I'm afraid of offending them, I'm so scared of how they're going to respond. So, you end up bowing to her rather than God. It's crazy — 1st Kings Chapter 19.

Look at Elijah when he calls down fire from heaven. He calls down fire from heaven, and it consumes the sacrifice, and then he puts 850 prophets of Baal to the sword. He did that, one of the greatest demonstrations of the power of God in human history, and then one woman who he never met threatened him, and he ran and was afraid for his life. Oh, and you can't just read the Bible. You have to read the Bible. The brother just called down fire from heaven. I'm not talking about praying that your car starts. I'm talking about calling down fire from heaven.

He was the man, and one woman who we never met threatens him, and he's running for his life, asking God to kill him. Talk about confusion. If she wanted to kill him, she would've sent an assassin, not a messenger, to tell him she was going to kill him because witchcraft flows through messengers. That's why you'll have that anxiety after you talk to the person on the phone that said, well, I really shouldn't say, but they said it anyway because they just gave you witchcraft and you ate it up. Hearers of Jezebel, listeners of Jezebel, be-

come messengers of Jezebel, become oper-
ators of Jezebel.

The spirit of fear will destroy lives and
destroy ministries. Watch what happens
when you're under the spirit of fear. This
is crazy. Fear creates discouragement,
which creates despair and causes you to
want to give up. Elijah called down fire
from heaven and then wanted to give up.
How do you have God use you so power-
fully? How does God do so much in your
life, and then all of a sudden, you want to
give up? It's witchcraft, and you've got to
be aware of it.

The Bible says this, look at 1st Kings
chapter 19:9, (paraphrased) God has to
say to Elijah, what are you doing here, Elijah, when he's running? Because anytime
you let Jezebel chase you out of your call,
your church, and your ministry will never
be in the right place that God wants for
you. You won't be in the place of obedience. You'll be in a place of disobedience,
and God had to say, what are you doing

here? The spirit of fear pushes you out of your destiny.

2. **Manipulation**

Number two, manipulation. She is undisciplined, so she must manipulate. How did she manipulate? Pouting, sulking, silent treatment, obsessiveness, tantrums, and sexual favor. She'll do anything that she can to manipulate you to do what you want. She will make you feel bad about her. She can cry at a moment's notice, and she can get emotional. She'll bring up the past. She'll do whatever it takes to manipulate you to do what she wants you to do. Let me say this, using the Bible to hurt people is witchcraft. When you try to use the Bible to curse people, that's witchcraft.

When you take the sword and bring it to your flesh, no one likes their flesh cut, but what I'm talking about is trying to curse people with God's word. Listen, God's word brings life, not death. God's word brings freedom, not imprisonment, not slavery. It brings life. Are you here with me today?

3. **Intimidation**

Number three, intimidation. She painted her eyes to make them look bigger. And, overall, to intimidate. How does she intimidate? She mocks. She talks down, she compares. You'll never be as good as me. You don't hold our name. You don't make us look good. You'll never be as good as your father. You'll never, and you'll never preach, you'll never minister. You won't do it. You won't go far. You'll never be successful. You're never going to be — intimidation, intimidation, intimidation.

4. **Domination**

And number four, intimidation creates complete and total domination. When you're dominated completely, it means you're controlled completely. You feel powerless to disagree with Jezebel. You feel a lower value. You feel less esteem. Every time you leave her presence, you feel small. I remember the times that I didn't even want to be awake anymore. I just wanted to go to sleep after I encountered a Jezebel interaction because it was such a dominating spirit that crushed my spirit. Listen, you must understand this.

Anytime you will create peace at any cost, it's spiritual terrorism. That you are so dominated, you will do anything that Jezebel wants you to do or tells you to do so that you don't cross this, so she's happy with you, so you're okay. You've given in to complete domination. That's what Ahab did. That's what we're seeing in America today. We see America be dominated by a foul spirit, an anti-Christ spirit, and what you need to do is understand that the battle is always over people. It's always fighting over the control of people, and please listen; if you are fighting people, you've already lost the battle because we're not fighting people, but we're fighting a spirit.

I believe that the Jezebel revelation empowered me to confront and embrace the gay community because it's the same strategy. We're facing a spirit in operation while loving people in the process. Listen, we're not at war with people. You can't put a person's name on it. It's a spirit that's in operation. We need to believe God for people's deliverance. We need to believe God for people's healing. We need to believe God for people's salvation. We need to believe God for people's freedom. And hear this, it's so hard, I'm just being real, not to take it personally when you are on the receiving end of Jezebel abuse and witchcraft.

That's when you start reflecting Jesus. He didn't defend himself. He could've. He could've stopped at any moment of the abuse. He could've stopped at any moment of the process. But what did he do? He surrendered to the will of the Father. Listen to me: how you defeat Jezebel isn't by fighting her pride with your pride. It's not being as strong as she is, and as spiritually tough as she is. If I'm honest with you, I still feel the effects of witchcraft, if I'm honest with you, it used to last months at a time, and every single day, I would feel the anxiety.

I'd feel the pressure, and I'd feel the fear. And it went from months to weeks, and then it went to days, later it went to hours.

The wonderful thing is when you learn how to fight spiritual warfare properly, and it works in all spiritual warfare. Seductive spirits work with ha-tred and racism, prejudice. It works with the spirit of offense where you know when your flesh rises, what witchcraft feels like, and how to respond spiritually to a spiritual battle. People are not the enemy. The enemy wants people. The enemy is the enemy, and the people of God need to brace ourselves to confront foul spirits and love people in the process.

Therefore, to stand our ground for young people, we don't want their lives destroyed. We don't want their marriages broken.

We want all people to come to the saving knowledge of Jesus Christ, a full life of repentance. We don't want to be them to be one of the people that Jesus said: go away from me, you doers of iniquity. I never knew you. We want to see repentance. We want to see deliverance. We want to see healing, and we want to see them set free. We want to see the God of restoration, restore lives, restore marriages, restore ministries. 1st Kings 18:11, when Elijah is standing in front of all of the people of Israel, and all of the false prophets, all of the activists, all of the professional preachers on one side, and all of the prophets and pastors are hiding.

In 1st Kings 18:11, Elijah said if God is God, serve him, but if Baal is God, then serve him. If God is God, then be a Christian if you serve the

God of the world and be a secularist. Jesus said I'd rather have you hot or cold. What if you're lukewarm, I'm going to spit you out. Who do you serve this day because you cannot submit to a Jezebel spirit and submit to the Lord at the same time? One of them is God, and Jezebel just wanted her God on the same altar. But Jesus is the name above all names. He is the highest authority.

Let me ask you this question. Is he the highest authority in your life? Is he the highest authority in your sexuality? Is he the highest authority in your emotions? Is he the highest authority in your political views? Is he the highest authority in your relationships? Is he the highest authority online for you? Is he the highest authority in the secret places for you? Is Jesus King of Kings and Lord of Lords in your life? I'm not talking about religion. I'm not talking about, even if you tithe, I'm talking about is He the King, is He the one that you kneel to, is he the one that you bow to?

Is he the one that you say, Lord, I'm going to give up my life. I'm going to abandon my flesh. I'm going pick up your cross, and I'm going to follow you with everything in me. If you tell me what I'm doing is wrong, I don't want to be right. God,

I want to be right in your eyes. I don't want to be right with men. I don't want to be popular on earth. I don't want the praise or the approval of men, but God, I want to please you with what I do, with how I live, with what I say, with what I watch, and with my being. I want to please you. Every head bowed, and every eye closed today.

Who do you serve today? I'm not going to ask you, do you have the Jezebel spirit. I'm saying, who's the Lord of your life because every spirit has to flee to the name of Jesus. Every demon has to bow. Even the demons recognize him as Lord. Even the world that worships a demon spirit. Their god serves and bows to our God. No one is like Jehovah. No one's strong in battle. No one's as mighty as him. There is no God like our God. But is he yours? Maybe you've been serving the Lord for years, but as the Lord of all, I didn't say is the Lord of most. You see because you cannot operate in the Jezebel spirit or any spirit when the Holy Spirit fully possesses you.

When you live in him and he in you, when you live and breathe and have your way in Him. When everything has to filter through your love for him, which is your obedience for him, changes the way you live, and it changes the way you worship. It changes the way you give, and it changes the way you work. It changes your public life, your social life, your private life, everything. Is he your Lord of all? Today, if you would say, I want to make Jesus the Lord of everything. I don't care if you've been serving the Lord for 30 years. I don't even know how many times I've done this. I do it almost daily. Lord, you know me, not the dressed up me. Not my performance, and not the good parts. You know everything. You know the dirty, and you know the rotten parts. You know my faults and failures, and you still call me son. You still love me.

Lord, I want a relationship with you. I want to be intimate with you. I don't want to be the one that says stay away from me. I want to come close to you. I want to know you. I want to know you like Moses said, I can't go unless you go with me. I want to know you. Like David said, you're my hiding place. You're my secret place. I want to know you. I want to know your mercies are new every morning. I want to hear your voice. God, I can't go without you. I need your voice. I need your presence. If that's you today, and you say, I need more of God. I need him to be the Lord of every area

– the Lord of my marriage, Lord of my children, Lord of my mind, Lord of my peace. I need more. If that's you, please stand to your feet, lift your hands all over this place and start asking for more.

Just start asking for more. Come on, just right now. Just start asking God for more, right where you are. Lord, we need more of you. Lift your voice right now and begin to cry to a Holy God. Lift your voice right now and begin to say, Father, would you forgive me, Lord, of anything that I've placed above you? Lord, would you forgive me? I repent God of anything that I have made God a priority in my life over you. Any access that I've given to the enemy, any avenue, any foothold, it's the small foxes that spoil the vine, God. I don't want anything in my life that doesn't please you. I don't want anything in my life that doesn't bring you glory, and that doesn't bring you honor. I want my secret place to be the same standard as my public life? Father, I want you to be Lord of all. Just ask Him right now.

If Jesus is Lord in your life or anyone's life, then Jezebel cannot be.

About the Author

Bill Vincent is no stranger to understanding the power of God. Not only has he spent over twenty years as a Minister with a strong prophetic anointing, he is now also an Apostle and Author with Revival Waves of Glory Ministries.

Bill offers a wide range of writings and teachings from deliverance, to experiencing presence of God and developing Apostolic cutting edge Church structure. Drawing on the power of the Holy Spirit through years of experience in Revival and Spiritual Sensitivity. Bill now focuses mainly on pursuing the Presence of God and maintaining Revival.

His books 50 and counting has since helped many people to overcome the spirits and curses of Satan.

Recommended Books

By Bill Vincent
Overcoming Obstacles
Glory: Pursuing God's Presence
Defeating the Demonic Realm
Increasing Your Prophetic Gift
Increase Your Anointing
Keys to Receiving Your Miracle
The Supernatural Realm
Waves of Revival
Increase of Revelation and Restoration
The Resurrection Power of God
Discerning Your Call of God
Apostolic Breakthrough
Glory: Increasing God's Presence
Love is Waiting – Don't Let Love Pass You
By
The Healing Power of God
Glory: Expanding God's Presence
Receiving Personal Prophecy
Signs and Wonders

Signs and Wonders Revelations
Children Stories
The Rapture
The Secret Place of God's Power
Building a Prototype Church
Breakthrough of Spiritual Strongholds
Glory: Revival Presence of God
Overcoming the Power of Lust
Glory: Kingdom Presence of God
Transitioning to the Prototype Church
The Stronghold of Jezebel
Healing After Divorce
A Closer Relationship With God
Cover Up and Save Yourself
Desperate for God's Presence
The War for Spiritual Battles
Spiritual Leadership
Global Warning
Millions of Churches
Destroying the Jezebel Spirit
Awakening of Miracles
Deception and Consequences Revealed
Are You a Follower of Christ
Don't Let the Enemy Steal from You!
A Godly Shaking
The Unsearchable Riches of Christ

Heaven's Court System
Satan's Open Doors
Armed for Battle
The Wrestler
Spiritual Warfare: Complete Collection
Growing In the Prophetic
Faith
The Angry Fighter's Story
Understanding Heaven's Court System
Restoration of the Soul
Spiritual Warfare Made Simple
Aligning With God's Promises
Deep Hunger
Beginning the Courts of Heaven
Breaking Curses
Writing and Publishing a Book
How to Write a Book
The Anointing
The Courts of Heaven

Web Site:
www.revivalwavesofgloryministries.com